The Old and The New

First produced and published in
England 1997 by
Dave Mallinson Publications
3 East View, Moorside, Cleckheaton, West
Yorkshire, England BD19 6LD
Telephone 01274 876388
Facsimile 01274 865208
E-mail mally@mally.com
Web http://www.mally.com
ISBN 1 899512 43 8
British Library cataloguing in publication data:
A catalogue record for this book is available
from the British Library
Set in Triplex
Music engraved in Petrucci using *Finale*
Page layout in *QuarkXPress*
Cover photograph looks over Rothbury to Cheviot
from Garleigh Moor and is © Robin Dunn
Photograph of Robin Dunn © Trish Turnbull
Data capture by Julie Taylor and David J Taylor
Design and data manipulation by David J Taylor
Unless in the public domain, all tunes and
dances are copyright © their respective owners
and used with permission
First printed in England 1997 by
The Digital Page Printing Company Limited
Telephone 0113 238 0815
All rights reserved

Dances & dance tunes
traditional & novel
from

Robin Dunn

DAVE MALLINSON PUBLICATIONS

Introduction & acknowledgements

This book has been put together in response to repeated requests for 'the dots' at *La Toque Bleu* performances over the last three or four years. It covers all of the album *The Rocking Horse* plus a wide selection from the repertoire I was playing before I started composing. In other words, my compositions and the music that inspired me to write them. Some of these other tunes are traditional and some from modern composers.

Rather than have the old and the new kept separate, I have mixed them together to make new sets. This has been a very enjoyable experience as it has given a new lease of life to one or two tunes which I hadn't played for some time.

Throughout the book I have tried to give some general idea of the influences and inspirations behind the types of tune I've written. On this opening page though, I'd like to make special mention of a handful of people who have profoundly affected the way I play and think about music.

Three fiddlers spring immediately to mind—Tony Corcoran, Chuck Fleming and Willy Taylor. I played with Chuck and Tony (along with my brother Martin Dunn and Alistair Anderson) in the *Steel Skies Band*. They are both extremely skilful fiddlers with differing styles and formidable as a team.

Willy Taylor has a wonderfully individual style of playing the fiddle which sounds quite straightforward but which is deceptively difficult to emulate. He has written some great tunes that are turning out to be real landmarks.

Joe Hutton has been an inspiration to all who met him—unfailingly calm and in control on stage and ever cheerful and buoyant off it. Sadly he passed away in the summer of 1996; he was a great effervescent character who was as loved as he was respected. He will be greatly missed.

Two accordionists who I occasionally get to sit in with and whose playing makes me want to dance, are John Dagg of *The Tillside Trio* and Bryce Anderson of *The Cheviot Ranters*. They both have a feel for the music which is rarely matched by the rest of us.

Finally the musician who was my first real inspiration—Willie Atkinson. I first heard Willie play shortly after I started playing dance music and that set the target! From then on I only ever wanted to make my mandolin sound like Willie's 'moothie'.

It is impossible to overstate the influence on my music of playing with musicians of this calibre; I feel their presence in most of what I do.

Obviously a great many more people have impressed and influenced me over the years and their names will be mentioned in the following pages; I thank them all and hope that they, as well as you, will enjoy the fruits of their influence.

R Dunn

Robin Dunn, August 1997

The tunes marked ❶ can be heard on the album *The Rocking Horse.*
The tunes marked ② can be heard on the album *Dunn—by his friends.*
Both albums can be obtained from either the publishers or Robin himself.

Index of tunes

Index of dances

The first tune that I ever wrote—or rather the first tune that I wrote and didn't immediately consign to the bin—was *Neil Smith's Waltz*. Neil is a very fine recorder player with whom I played lots of duets in the late seventies and early eighties. We won all the local 'pairs' competitions—Morpeth, Newcastleton, Rothbury and Alnwick—several times and this was the opening tune of our set the first time we won at Alnwick.

It is teamed here with *Trish's Waltz*, a relatively recent composition, named for Trish Turnbull without whose support I could not have written this book.

Neil Smith's Waltz

Trish's Waltz

The Old and The New

Reels, rants and marches

The terms *reels, rants* and *marches* are used to separate tunes which can sometimes have more similarities than differences; with some, it is difficult to find the dividing line. In recent years, particularly when making up sets for my weekly dance music workshop at Gateshead, I have frequently combined reels and marches, partly for the contrasting texture and also simply to give the fingers a rest if the reel is a lively one. A good example of this would be to follow *The De'il Amang The Tailors* with *The Barren Rocks of Aden*.

I tend to think of rants as simply tunes that sound good at a speed at which dancers can comfortably rant...this is perhaps more confining than any definition which might apply to reels or marches. A tune written as a rant may also, of course, sound good when played as a reel but the reverse of this does not always apply.

I have arranged the tunes here according to the way I use them at the present time; you may think fit to slow them down, speed them up, or give them a little cosmetic surgery to better suit them to your purposes. Feel free.

The Walkerville Reel

Robin Dunn's Compliments to Chuck Fleming

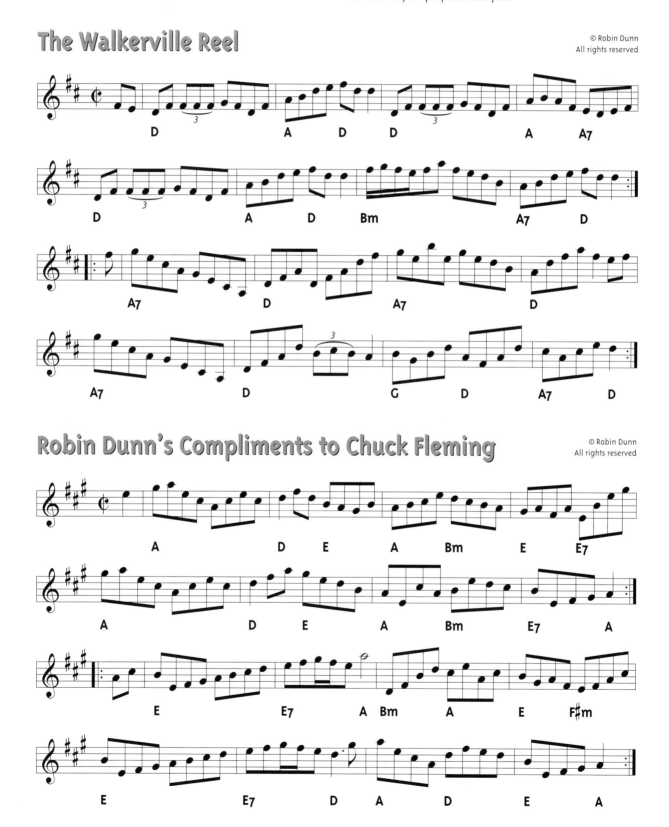

The Old and The New

The Meeting of the Waters

Traditional

A   D   A   A   Bm   F♯m   E7   A

D   A   A   A D A   A   D   A

A   Bm   F♯m E7   A   D   A   A   E7   A D A

Andrew's March

Traditional

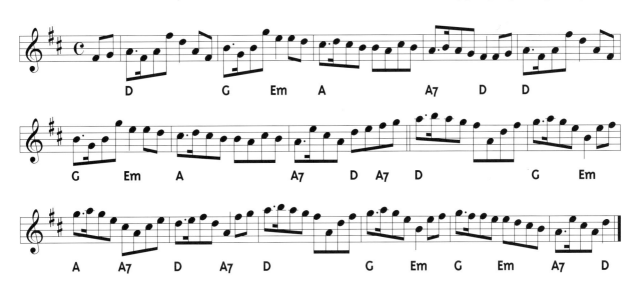

D   G   Em   A   A7   D   D

G   Em   A   A7   D A7   D   G   Em

A   A7   D   A7   D   G   Em G   Em   A7   D

The Eight-thirty March

G   Bm   Em   G   Am   G   C Bm Am D7   G   Bm

Em   G   Am   G   Am D7 G   Am   D7   C Cm G

A   A7   D Am D7   G   Bm   Em   G   Am   G   Am D7 G

The Old
The New

I'd lean towards playing these three tunes as rants. I learned *Whinham's* and *Roxburgh Castle* many years ago and they are still very popular—you can hear them almost every month at the Alnwick Pipers' Society meetings.

Whinham's Reel

Composed by Robert Whinham

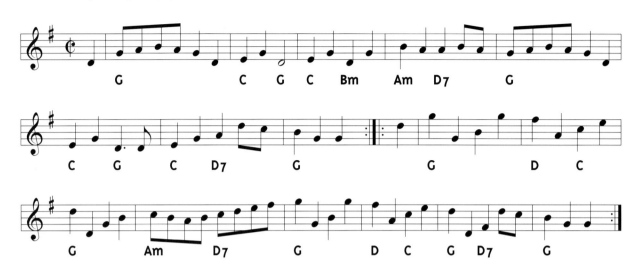

Two Steps Forward and One Step Back

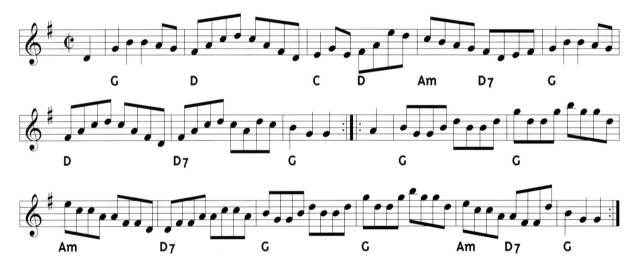

Roxburgh Castle

Traditional

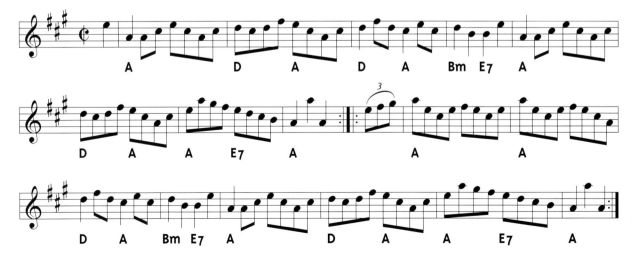

The Old *and* The New

A set of 16-bar tunes which work well at rant speed. The first is French-Canadian and I'm told it's meant to go faster than a rant.

But then again, lots of tunes which get played fast sound good when played a little slower.

Traditional

La Toque Bleu

The Battery

The Cockroach

The Trip to Dryburgh

7

The Old
The New

Dotted reels

Dotted reels is a term I use to describe the sort of reels which sound like speeded-up hornpipes. Some Irish players have this kind of style but I'm thinking here of something more pronounced, the clearest example being heard in the playing of Willy Taylor. Willy has written some very good reels, all in the same distinctive style.

The first tune of Willy's that I learned was *Nancy Taylor's Reel*; this was part of a set that I played with Neil Smith in one of the local competitions. We played it dead straight though and although I was enjoying playing it enormously, I began to feel that it didn't have the same magic that Willy's playing gave it. I then set about learning to play it in his style—the way he wrote it—and I'm still learning.

It has been my great privilege for the last five years to play in the same band as my favourite piano player, Sue Morgan. She is certainly the most adventurous, creative and dynamic player that I've ever come across in Britain. Her style comes directly from the playing styles of New England and Cape Breton and she is the single most significant influence on my playing and composing today. *The Telephonist* is named for her as it is what she does for a living.

Nancy Taylor's Reel

Variation

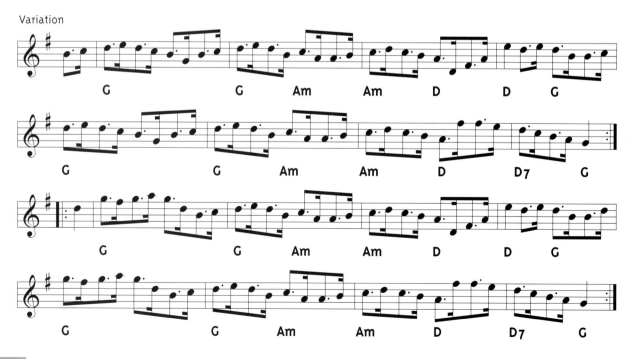

The Old
and
The New

The Kipper

The Pearl Wedding

The Telephonist

The Old
The New

New England dance music

My first contact with this music was from hearing a tape of *New England Chestnuts* which Alistair put on during a break in *Steel Skies* rehearsals. I took an immediate liking to it and borrowed it—along with a tape of George Wilson and Selma Kaplan.

Their reels are particularly stylish; they tend to be of the heavily dotted variety (like hornpipes) and have the distinct punctuations of good dance music. Rodney Miller actually described them to me as "speeded up hornpipes" and indeed they do play some English and Irish hornpipes as reels. (Incidentally, Willy Taylor also told me that *Nancy Taylor's Reel* started out as a hornpipe).

I was by this time well primed for learning some more tunes in this format having already pilfered half of Willy's repertoire, so I learned most of the tunes on the tapes in no time at all...well, the easy ones. Then in frustration at not having any more to go at, I started writing some of my own in the same mode.

Ironically, *The Summerhill Hornpipe* works well as a hornpipe.

The untitled tune is transcribed from a tape recording made in New England and is part of a set of dance reels. Whoever gave the tape to me (and why) has unfortunately been lost in the mists of time, along with the name of the tune. However, you may recognise the first half of the tune as being the same as the first half of *The Navvie on the Line*, a favourite hornpipe on this side of the Atlantic.

The Summerhill Hornpipe

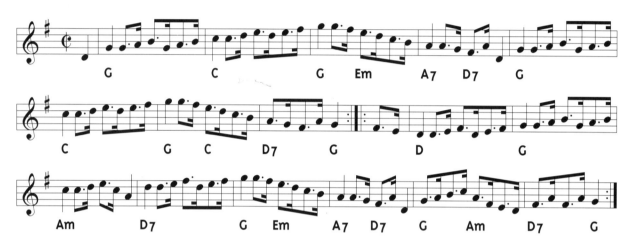

Untitled Reel

Traditional

The Reciprocal Reel
© Robin Dunn

A longways dance for as many as will. Although the dance was written with dotted reels in mind, you could do it to any reels, jigs or marches.

A1 1st couple lead down the set for 4 steps and 'box the gnat', come back and cast one place. 2nd couple move up.

A2 Northumbrian-style ladies' chain across the set and back.

B1 Do-si-do partner, do-si-do contrary.

B2 Set twice to partner and swing. Finish on own side.

Mona Cameron

Traditional

Ross's Reel

Traditional

The Reciprocal Reel

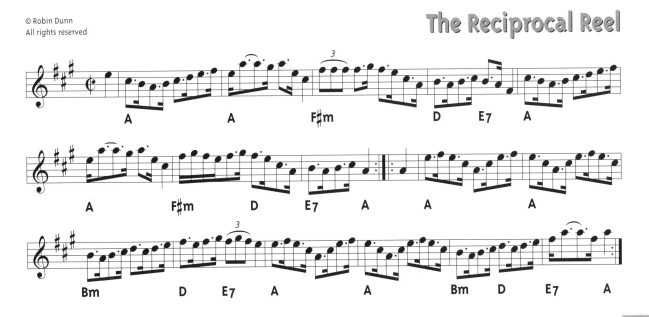

The Old
The New

Rodney on the Dance Floor

Le Reel des Jeunes Marie

Traditional

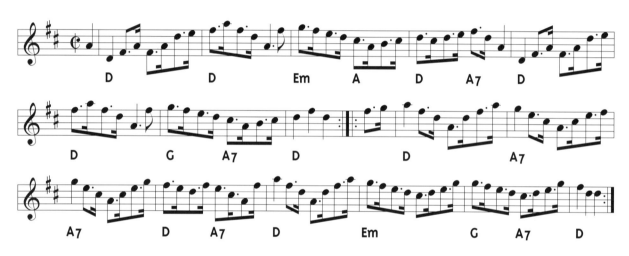

Chris and Sara's Tune

Bernhervie Picnic

The Broken Chanter

I have come across three different versions of the second half of Quigley's; I'm not claiming this as the definitive one, I just happen to like it.

Traditional

Quigley's

One of my own favourites this one. It was named for the Rosecroft School Band and their excellent all-singing, all-dancing, melodeon-playing headmaster, Adrian Hopley.

Written originally in D on the fiddle and later changed to C to suit Richard Adamson, our melodeon player. I like it best on two mandolins.

The Rosecroft Rant

Mrs Milligan was learned from Norman Foster who played second box in *The Cheviot Ranters* and now leads *The Glen Aln Band.*

Traditional

Mrs Milligan

Robin's Rant

The Cheviot Rant
© George Mitchell

A Sicilian Circle dance devised by George Mitchell of *The Cheviot Ranters.*

A1 (Ranting) Step twice to opposite and 1/2 right hand turn. Step twice to partner and 1/2 left hand turn.

A2 Repeat A1.

B1 (Walking) Right hand star and left hand star.

B2 (Ranting) Forward and back, pass on as couple, men passing left shoulder.

I originally wrote *Pam and Julia's March* in E flat. I've no idea why: just an experiment I think. I had an inkling though, that Pam and Julia might not be as impressed as I was with this feat

so before I gave them it, I transposed it: first into G then into D.

It transpires that the G version nicely fits the pipes and the low notes in the D version sound good on the fiddle.

© Dave Mallinson Publications 1997

The Barren Rocks of Aden

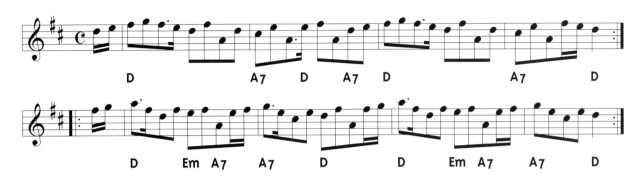

Miss Linda MacFarlane

The New March

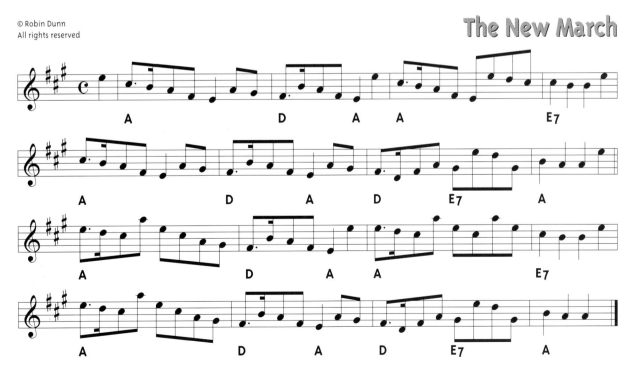

The Old
and
The New

The Jigsaw

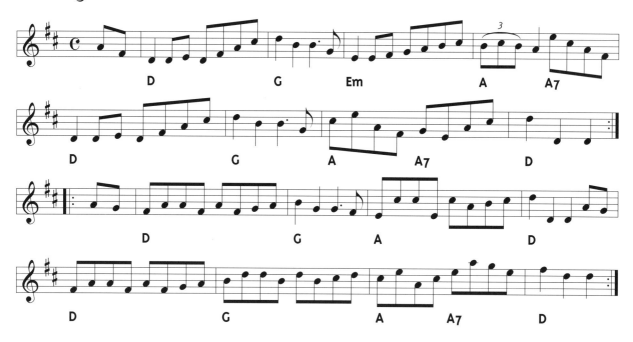

Wallsend Memorial Hall

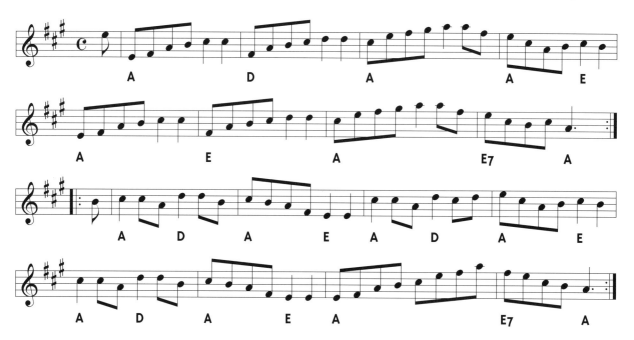

The Rifleman
Traditional

A ranting dance in *Becket* formation, that is, longways set with couples facing couples across the dance.

A1 Forward two rant steps and back; forward again and gents, with cross-hand hold, bring the opposite lady round to partner's place (man turning leftwards).

A2 Repeat this figure, bringing partner back to place.

B1 Northumbrian ladies' chain.

B2 Top two couples dance down the set (this can be galloping, swinging, circling, or whatever takes your fancy), the rest move up.

Written as solo reels we still nevertheless use them for dances.
We play the first one AABB AABA which gives the best ending.

The Cauld Pool

The Back Braes

The Brickie

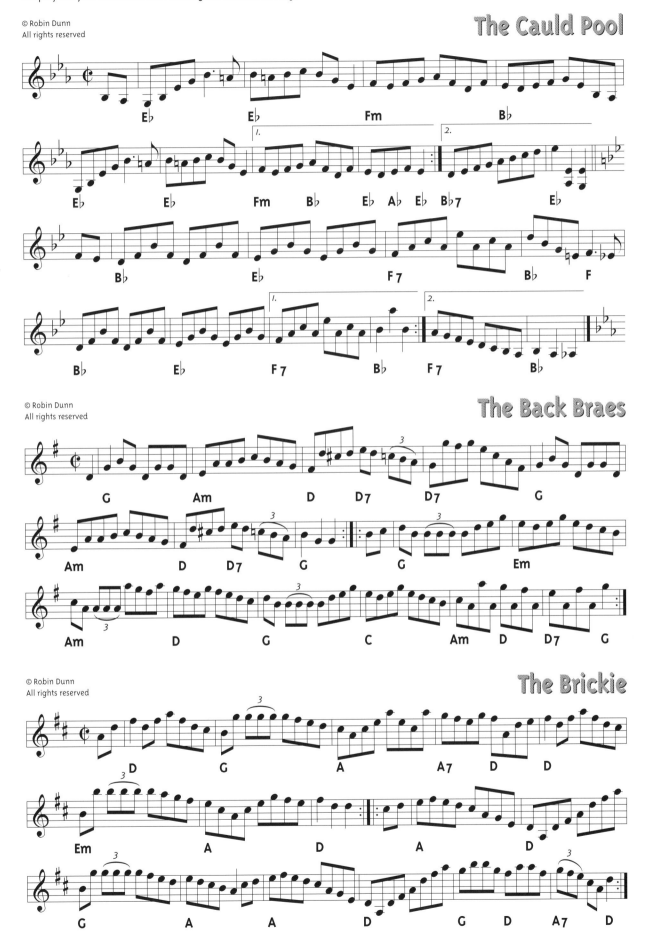

The Old
and
The New

A few years ago Pete Woods approached me with the idea of doing a 'northern' version of Peter Bellamy's ballad opera, *The Transports*. Pete was going to produce it and asked me to arrange the music: I ended up having to completely re-write it as all of our cast sang in different keys to those of the original version.

It was a labour of love, however, since the quality of the original material was excellent and also the cast that Pete assembled were a joy to work with. The singers were Jim

Mageean, Benny Graham, Johnny Handel, Dory Dixon, Alan Fitzsimmons and Pete himself. Playing the tunes always brings back fond memories.

These two started off as themes of the linking passages and I liked them so much that I felt that I had to develop them individually. The first is named for Joe Scurfield of *The Old Rope String Band* and the second, as you have probably already worked out, was part of the overture to the opera.

Joe Scurfield's Favourite

The Overture

© Dave Mallinson Publications 1997

The title of the first tune shown here came from a wonderful malapropism uttered by a friend of mine—to whom I'll be kind and leave nameless—during a conversation about science-fiction films.

The Famous White Pudding refers to part of a mixed grill offered as a raffle prize at a local pub; the white pudding was passed around the room until finally being accepted by me and becoming somehow notorious in the process.

The Day of the Griffiths

The Famous White Pudding

The Old and The New

Hornpipes

I wrote *Mr Welch's* and *The Swing Bridge* after hearing the *Gas Mark V* treatment of *William Kimber's Double Take* on their album *In the Kitchen*.

When *La Toque Bleu* recorded these on the album *The Rocking Horse,* Richard Adamson led the arrangement on a one-row melodeon with all four stops out (or is that in?) which resulted in a lot of people taking the track for Cajun music.

William Kimber's Double Take

Traditional

Mr Welch's Favourite

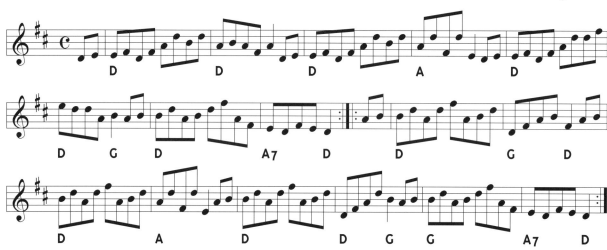

The Swing Bridge

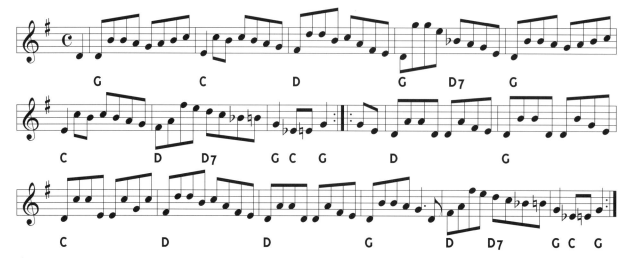

Snod's Edge is a small village in County Durham where we often play for barn dances. It became famous recently when the local gardening club appeared on the BBC's *Gardeners' Question Time.*

Snod's Edge

Opening Time

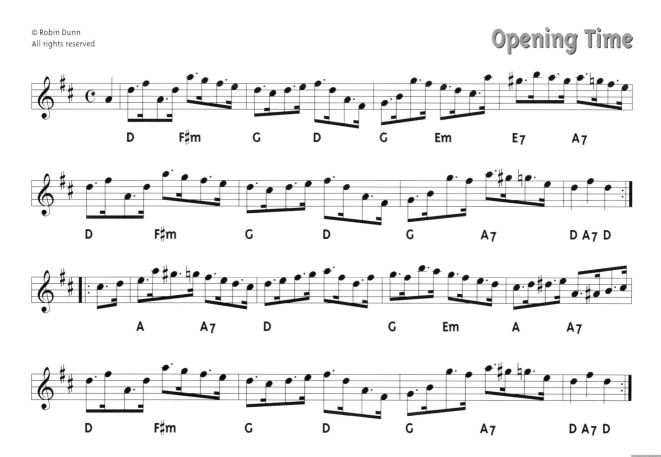

The Old and The New

I'll Get Wedded in my Auld Claes

Traditional

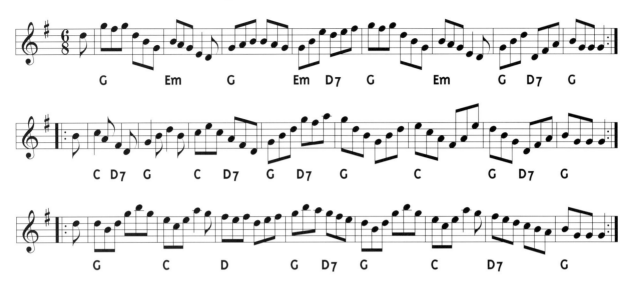

48-bar jigs

For the first four or five years that I played in dance bands it seemed to me that there were only four 48-bar jigs in existence and I became heartily sick of the sound of them. There were two widely known ones, *Merrily Kissed the Quaker* and *Blarney Pilgrim*, plus two more local ones, *The Random Jig* and *I'll Get Wedded In Me Auld Claes*. Excellent tunes all of them, but I'd played them just too many times.

Eventually, when I needed to assemble some easy 48-bar sets for my weekly workshop and bearing in mind that *The Random* and *I'll Get Wedded* are a bit on the difficult side, I realised that I was down to two. So the first ones that I wrote were born of a great frustration.

An added spur was that the workshop band, *The Redheughers*, played for a monthly ceilidh and our regular caller (and founder of The Gateshead Ceilidh Club) Eddie Upton, had an unfathomable depth of 48-bar dances in his repertoire.

So, the first two I wrote were called *The Redheugh Library Jig* and *The Tuesday Night Jig* and are printed in the *Folkworks Ceilidh Band Pack* and also in *The Morpeth Rant* by Matt Seattle.

We met at the Redheugh Library every Tuesday (hence the titles) except for the first Tuesday of each month which is when the ceilidh club was held. The club and the workshop are still thriving so do please visit us if you are in the area. We now meet at Gateshaed Central Library.

The Rocking Horse was the perfectly good name of a pub in Hexham which was changed, like so many others in the name of marketing strategy, to something less memorable.

The Rocking Horse

Two-steps

Old-time couple dances are still very popular in rural Northumberland. Most dances are still held without a caller, the programme comprising mostly couple dances broken up perhaps by the inclusion of an *Eightsome Reel, The Dashing White Sergeant* and *Strip The Willow* (the version locally popular being called *Drops Of Brandy* and danced to hornpipes!). Very occasionally there might be a *Morpeth Rant* if enough people request it.

The tunes played for the two-steps tend to be in six-eight and having three parts, with at least one part being in a different key to the other two. Quite often only the one tune is played per dance, which contrasts dramatically with the normal tradition in the north of playing three or four tunes per dance and the arrangement of parts might be something like AABACABCA. At the end of each dance there is usually a short pause whilst the band find a different tune then they repeat the dance.

These kind of tunes can also of course be used as straight 48s, ie ABC,ABC etc.

The Summerhill Two-step

The Eva Three-step

Traditional

A couple dance done to two-steps.

A1 Walk forward three steps and clap hands.

Change places with partner (3 steps) and clap hands.

Change places with partner again and clap hands.

Meet partner and take a ballroom hold.

A2 *Either* take 4 steps towards the middle of the room (man pull/lady push) and back again,

Or chassay two steps anti-clockwise and back again.

Then dance around with pas-de-bas step.

© Dave Mallinson Publications 1997

The Old and The New

Sunflowers

The Belle of the Ball
Traditional

A dance for lines of three people which goes well to two-steps.

Although meant for lines comprising two women and one man, I always do it with lines of any composition—which makes it even more fun.

A1 Lines go anti-clockwise round the room for 4 steps and then backwards for 4. The lines then reverse direction thus: they raise each others' hands to make arches, then the one on the right goes through the left-hand arch, taking the middle person with them. As this is happening, the left-most person walks (with upraised arm) to the other end of the line, very much like doing half a right-hand turn.

A2 Repeat the above, going clockwise first. All will now be facing anti-clockwise again.

B1 Join hands in circles of 3 and go left for 8 steps and then right.

B2 Straighten the lines and do reels of three (figures of eight) at the end of which the middle person moves on to the next line in front, ready to start again.

Rapper jigs

Some years ago *La Toque Bleu* and *The Addison Rapper Team* visited Belgium. It was a gem of a trip: wonderful people (the Belgians, not us), wonderful food and the beer-drinkers amongst us (only one or two), were on cloud nine.

Out of it came two tunes with really imaginative titles.

The Newcastle Kingsmen's Visit to Sicily commemorates another memorable trip abroad: warm Italian sunshine in the middle of February, magnificent food, panoramic views of the Mediterranean coastline, marble temples, almond blossom, streets full of brightly costumed dancers...just lie back and think of Sicily.

The Addison Rapper Team's Visit to Belgium

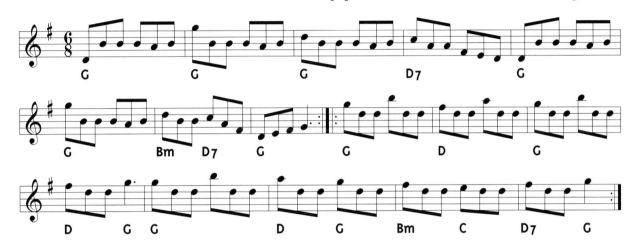

Phillipe Dumont's Visit to England

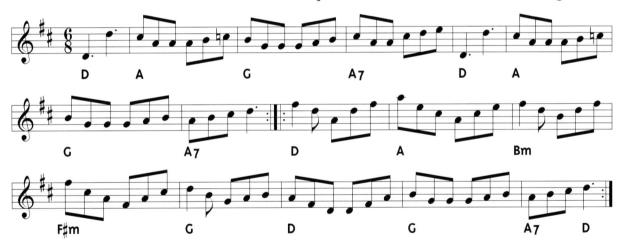

The Newcastle Kingsmen's Visit to Sicily

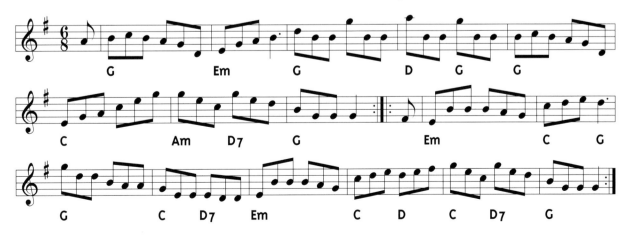

© Dave Mallinson Publications 1997

The Old
The New

Hollins' Jig was written to go with a dance of the same name which was devised by Eddie Upton during his time as Folk Musician In Residence at Gateshead. It can be found in his book *Caedmon Capers*.

I Won't do the Work

Traditional

Hollins' Jig

Ann Frazer MacKenzie

Traditional

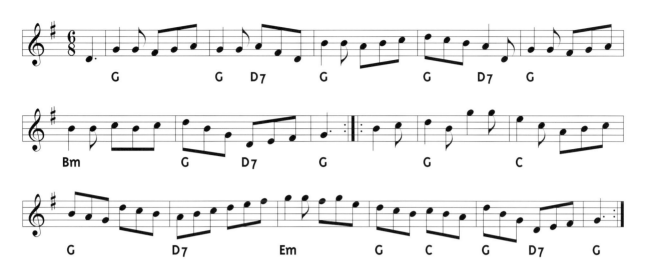

Barley Mow Village Hall

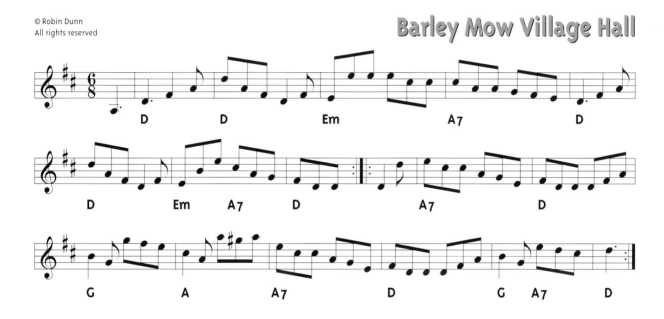

Emma's Liquorice Boats

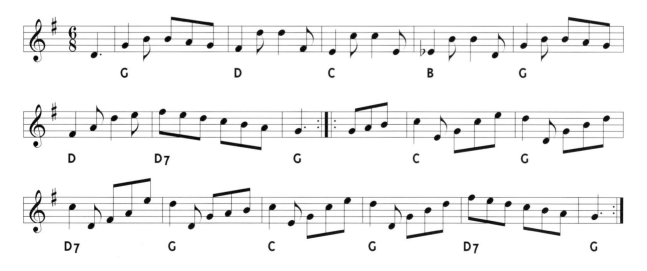

The Old
The New

Something a little slower...a tune for a tree. Written in the hope that it would induce a more co-operative attitude in the fruit department! The problem was a shortage of plums, or more specifically, no plums at all. It did seem to perk up a bit last year but then it was attacked by bullfinches and stripped of all its fruit buds. This year sees its last chance...

The Plum Tree

A slow waltz. The title of this tune comes from the name of a variety of fuschia that I had growing on my windowsill at the time that I wrote it. Unfortunately, I planted it out in the garden for the summer and forgot to bring it in for the winter; so now instead of being a celebration, it has become a lament. What a sad story.

Cloverdale Pearl

The Old and The New

A last waltz—and a magic moment. This was my latest composition at the time of going to print. It was written for Alistair and Liz Anderson's 25th wedding anniversary at which *La Toque Bleu* played the music.

Sue and I launched into the tune without any prior announcement and almost immediately Liz crossed the floor and got Ali up to dance. There were only the two of them, no-one else joined in. It was a wonderfully romantic moment. It was also probably the best reaction to any tune that this composer has ever written.

Liz and Ali's Anniversary Waltz